Text Structures

All About Tigers

A Description Text

Phillip Simpson

CP/4

Raintree is an imprint of Capstone Global Library Limited, a company incorporated in England and Wales having its registered office at 7 Pilgrim Street, London, EC4V 6LB – Registered company number: 6695582

www.raintreepublishers.co.uk
myorders@raintreepublishers.co.uk

Text © Capstone Global Library Limited 2015
First published in hardback in 2014
Paperback edition published in 2015
The moral rights of the proprietor have been asserted.

Edited by Diyan Leake and Kathryn Clay
Designed by Steve Mead
Picture research by Tracy Cummins
Production by Helen McCreath
Originated by Capstone Global Library Ltd
Printed and bound in China by Leo Paper Group

ISBN 978 1 406 28350 1 (hardback)
18 17 16 15 14
10 9 8 7 6 5 4 3 2 1

ISBN 978 1 406 28356 3 (paperback)
19 18 17 16 15
10 9 8 7 6 5 4 3 2 1

British Library Cataloguing in Publication Data
A full catalogue record for this book is available from the British Library.

Acknowledgements
We would like to thank the following for permission to reproduce photographs: Getty Images: Keren Su, 9; Naturepl.com: © Anup Shah, 17, © David Woodfall, 16, © Florian Möllers, 23, © Mark Carwardine, 21, © Nick Garbutt, 10, © Staffan Widstrand, 5, © Vivek Menon, 24, © Vladimir Medvedev, 14; Shutterstock: David Evison, 20, Dennis Donohue, 8 left, Erika Kusuma Wardani, 18, hxdbzxy, 26, Jakub Krechowicz, 29 (notebook), John Dorado, 6, katielittle, 19, Michal Ninger, 7, neelsky, 8 right, Nikolay Tonev, 15, Ohishiapply, 28, Tatiana Morozova, 27, urfin , 29 (pen), Vladimir Korostyshevskiy, 25, Volodymyr Burdiak, 4; Wikimedia Commons: Dave Pape, 11.

Cover photograph reproduced with permission of Naturepl.com, © Andy Rouse.

Artistic effects
Shutterstock: Anan Kaewkhammul, Livijus Raubickas, Olga Kovalenko, Peshkova, Roman Sotola.

Contents

The text in this book has been organized using the description text structure. Descriptions use language to build a picture in the reader's mind. To find out more about writing using descriptions, see page 28.

Some words are shown in bold, **like this**. You can find out what they mean by looking in the glossary.

What is a tiger?

A tiger is a large, four-legged **mammal**. It is the largest cat in the world. Unlike lions, tigers do not live in groups. They are solitary animals and live alone. They are generally **nocturnal**, which means they are active at night.

Tigers are the largest of all the big cats.

The tiger is very popular in Asian cultures. It is considered the king of beasts and is often used as a symbol for royalty. The tiger is so popular that it is the national animal of India, Bangladesh, Malaysia and South Korea.

Tigers are sometimes pictured on artwork with gods and goddesses.

What tigers look like

Tigers have orange fur with dark stripes and white bellies. Their colour helps them hide so that other animals can't see them. This is known as **camouflage**. Tigers have very long whiskers. Males usually have longer whiskers than females.

A tiger's fur blends in with its surroundings.

A tiger's roar can be heard over a long distance.

Tiger claws are sharp and deadly. They use them to snatch and kill their **prey**. Tigers have the longest canine teeth of any cat. Tigers can weigh more than three adult men. From the tip of its nose to the tip of its tail, a tiger can be as long as 3.4 metres (11 feet).

Types of tigers

There are nine subspecies, or types, of tigers. The six surviving subspecies are the Bengal, Indochinese, Malayan, Sumatran, Siberian and South China tiger. They look very similar and have the same recognizable orange and black striped fur. The main differences are in their sizes and weights.

Siberian tiger

Sumatran tiger

Most tigers are easily recognized by their orange and black fur.

There used to be three more subspecies of tiger, but they are now **extinct**. Some of the surviving subspecies are **endangered**, or at risk of becoming extinct themselves. The South China tiger has not been seen in the wild for 25 years. Scientists think it is probably extinct in the wild.

South China tigers are only found in zoos.

Colourful tigers

Most tigers are orange and black, but they can come in other colours. Tigers sometimes have white or golden fur, although it is uncommon. White tigers are rare and mainly found in zoos.

The white tiger is usually larger than orange tigers.

The golden tiger is extinct in the wild.

Golden tigers are even rarer than white tigers. Their fur is a light gold colour and is generally thicker than the fur of other tigers. Like white tigers, golden tigers are usually larger than other tigers. There are very few golden tigers in **captivity**. The last wild one was killed in India many years ago.

Where tigers are found

Tigers used to be found all over Asia. Today they are only found in a few countries. The Bengal tiger is found in India, Nepal, Bhutan, and Bangladesh. The Sumatran tiger is found on the Indonesian island of Sumatra. The Malayan tiger lives in Malaysia, and the Siberian tiger lives in the cold, snowy forests of Siberia.

Map showing distribution of tigers in the wild

Tiger numbers have fallen significantly since 1900.

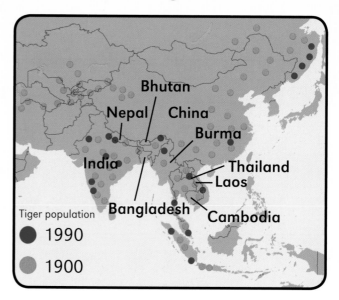

Bhutan

Nepal / China

Burma

India

Thailand

Laos

Bangladesh

Cambodia

Tiger population

● 1990

● 1900

Map showing suspected location of South China tigers

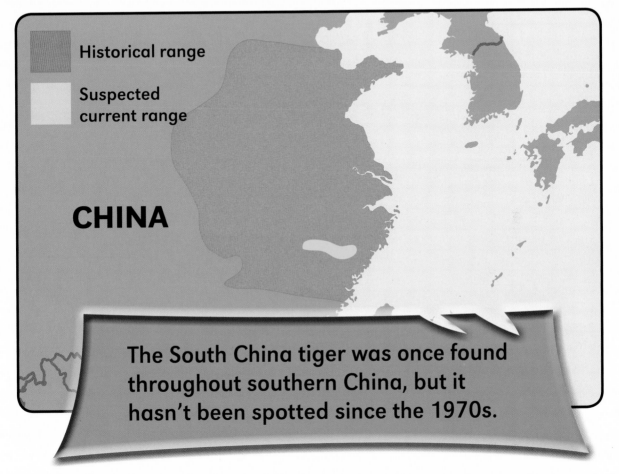

Historical range

Suspected current range

CHINA

The South China tiger was once found throughout southern China, but it hasn't been spotted since the 1970s.

The Indochinese tiger can still be found in parts of Cambodia, China, Laos, Burma, Thailand, and Vietnam. The South China tiger is thought to be extinct in the wild, but some believe there may be a few left. A few still survive in captivity.

Where tigers live

Tigers live in many types of **habitats**, but most live in forests. They prefer forests because the colour of their fur helps them hide from prey.

Camouflaged fur keeps tigers well hidden.

A tree branch makes a perfect lookout.

Some tigers, such as Siberian tigers, live in areas that are more open. In order to survive, their habitats must have water, animals to hunt and dens or caves in which to have their young. Large, hollow trees are sometimes used by tigers as places to rest and sleep.

Hunting and diet

Tigers are known as **carnivores** because they are meat eaters. Tigers hunt mostly at night. They usually hide in the forest and **ambush** their prey. Their powerful jaws grab prey by the throat and kill it.

Tigers sneak up on their prey.

Chital are common prey for the Bengal tiger.

The tiger's favourite prey include deer and wild boar or pigs. But tigers will eat birds, monkeys and even fish. Unlike some other large cats, they are comfortable in water and often **stalk** prey there.

Tiger cubs and lifespan

Tigers like to live alone. A male and female will **mate** and then separate. They are unlikely to meet again until the next mating season. A tiger cub will be born about 100 days after mating. Most females will have one to six cubs, but two or three is most common.

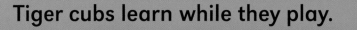
Tiger cubs learn while they play.

Tiger cubs stay with their
mothers for two years.

Female tigers raise their cubs alone. Cubs will
stay with their mother for about two years. Their
mother will teach them how to hunt during this
time. They are usually able to hunt by themselves
after a year. Tigers can live up to 26 years.

Conservation

Tigers used to be far more common. Today there are not many tigers left in the wild. This is because their natural habitat is being destroyed by humans. Without their natural habitats, tigers have no way to get food and water and no safe place to raise their young.

With their habitats destroyed, tigers are often found near farmlands and roads.

Chopping down trees destroys tigers' habitat.

As the human population increases, more room is needed to grow crops and build houses. People chop down forests to make way for houses and farms. These forests are the tigers' habitat. Places where tigers can be safe are known as reserves. These are places where tigers can live safely.

Numbers

At the start of the 1900s, it was thought that there were around 100,000 tigers in the wild. Today there are around 3,000 tigers left in the wild. Each year this number continues to fall. If humans do nothing to help, the tiger is in danger of becoming extinct.

Graph showing tiger decline

Tiger numbers have fallen greatly in the last 100 years.

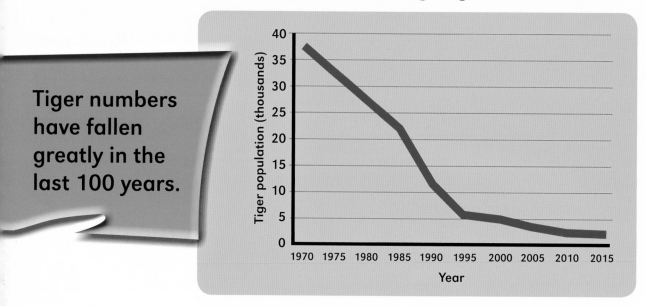

Almost half the tigers alive in the wild live in India. Bangladesh and Malaysia have the second highest population of tigers, with about 500. An **estimated** 45 tigers are left in China.

Today most tigers found in China are in zoos.

Humans and tigers

Humans and tigers do not mix well. Humans are dangerous to tigers because they destroy the tigers' natural habitats and hunt them for sport. In the past, tiger skins were sold for a lot of money. In parts of Asia, tiger parts are still used as medicine.

Tiger skins are sometimes used as rugs.

Shrinking habitats sometimes force tigers to feed on livestock.

Tigers are also a danger to humans. Because of the destruction of their habitats, tigers are often seen near villages as they hunt cows, goats and other livestock. Tigers sometimes hunt and kill humans when their usual prey cannot be found. As ambush **predators**, they can be incredibly dangerous to humans in the wild.

Captivity

Tigers are found in zoos all around the world and are very popular with visitors. Having tigers in zoos is one way to ensure the species doesn't become extinct. Breeding tigers in zoos is slowly helping to increase their numbers. Some tigers bred in zoos have been released into the wild.

Tigers can live safely in zoos.

Tiger cubs have a high survival rate in zoos.

There are several thousand tigers in zoos. Most are found in China and the United States. Hundreds more are kept as pets. However, this can be dangerous for both humans and tigers. Most tigers in zoos are well cared for and have large cages or enclosures.

Explanation of text structure

This book has been written using the **description** text structure. Descriptions say what a person or thing is like. Descriptions include adjectives and nouns. Adjectives are describing words. They say what things are like. Nouns are naming words. They say what things are called.

Tigers' claws are very sharp and deadly. They use them to seize and kill their prey. They have the longest canine teeth of any cat. Tigers can weigh more than three adult men. From the tip of its nose to the tip of its tail, the Siberian tiger can be as long as 3.3 metres (11 feet).

Nouns
Adjectives

Now you could try using the **description** text structure to write about:
- a caterpillar turning into a butterfly
- your favourite animal or pet
- a special place you visited on holiday

Glossary

ambush a surprise attack

camouflage the natural colouring or body shape that allows an animal to blend in with its surroundings

captivity to be held in a small area such as a zoo

carnivore an animal that eats meat

endangered close to dying out

estimate to make a guess about the amount, size, or value of something

extinct no longer existing

habitat a natural home for an animal or plant

mammal an animal that has hair on its body and feeds its babies with milk from the mother

mate to come together to produce babies

nocturnal active at night

predator an animal that hunts and eats other animals

prey an animal that is hunted and eaten by other animals

stalk to follow silently and slowly

Find out more

Books

Tigers (Amazing Animals), Valerie Bodden
  (Franklin Watts, 2012)

Tigers (Amazing Animal Hunters), Sally Morgan
  (Amicus, 2011)

Tigers (Usborne Beginners), James Maclaine (Usborne, 2012)

Websites

gowild.wwf.org.uk/asia
Visit the World Wildlife Fund's Go Wild section to learn
more about tigers and where they live.

www.bbc.co.uk/nature/life/Tiger
This website has some amazing videos of tigers.

www.kids.nationalgeographic.com/kids/animals/
creaturefeature/tiger
Learn more about tigers on National Geographic's website.

Index